ALTO SAX

Hymns FOR THE Master

15 FAVORITE HYMNS FOR SOLO PERFORMANCE

PLAYBACK+
Speed • Pitch • Balance • Loop

To access audio, visit:
www.halleonard.com/mylibrary

Enter Code
3688-1522-0392-7787

ISBN 978-0-7935-7188-8

Visit Hal Leonard Online at
www.halleonard.com

World headquarters, contact:
Hal Leonard
7777 West Bluemound Road
Milwaukee, WI 53213
Email: info@halleonard.com

In Europe, contact:
Hal Leonard Europe Limited
1 Red Place
London, W1K 6PL
Email: info@halleonardeurope.com

In Australia, contact:
Hal Leonard Australia Pty. Ltd.
4 Lentara Court
Cheltenham, Victoria, 3192 Australia
Email: info@halleonard.com.au

ALL HAIL THE POWER OF JESUS' NAME

Alto Sax

Traditional

JOYFUL, JOYFUL WE ADORE THEE

Alto Sax

Traditional

TAKE MY LIFE AND LET IT BE

Traditional

Alto Sax

GOD OF GRACE AND GOD OF GLORY

Text by HARRY EMERSON FOSDICK
Music by JOHN HUGHES

Alto Sax

6

BE THOU MY VISION

Alto Sax

Traditional Irish

CROWN HIM WITH MANY CROWNS

Alto Sax

Traditional

I LOVE THEE

Alto Sax

Traditional

ALL CREATURES OF OUR GOD AND KING

Alto Sax

Traditional

SAVIOR LIKE A SHEPHERD LEAD US

Traditional

Alto Sax

MY FAITH LOOKS UP TO THEE

Alto Sax

Traditional

JESUS SHALL REIGN WHERE'ER SUN

Words by ISAAC WATTS
Music by JOHN HATTON

Alto Sax

THIS IS MY FATHER'S WORLD

Alto Sax

Words by **MALTBIE BABCOCK**
Traditional Music

FOR THE BEAUTY OF THE EARTH

Text by FOLLIOT S. PIERPOINT
Music by CONRAD KOCHER

Alto Sax

WHEN I SURVEY THE WONDROUS CROSS

Words by LOWELL MASON
Music by ISAAC WATTS

Alto Sax

AMAZING GRACE

Words by JOHN NEWTON
Traditional American Melody

Alto Sax